WITHDRAWN

TIMELINES

1940s

by
Jane Duden

CRESTWOOD HOUSE

New York

Library of Congress Cataloging In Publication Data
Duden, Jane.
　　1940s / by Jane Duden.
　　p. cm. — (Timelines)
　　Includes index.
　　Summary: History, trivia, and fun through photographs and articles present life
in the United States between 1940 and 1949.
　　ISBN 0-89686-475-8
　　1. United States—History—1933-1945—Juvenile literature. 2. World War, 1939-
1945—United States—Juvenile literature. 3. History, Modern—20th century—
Juvenile literature. 4. United States—History—1945-1953—Juvenile literature. [1.
United States—History—1933-1945—Miscellanea. 2. United States—History—1945-
1953—Miscellanea.] I. Title. II. Title: Nineteen forties. III. Series: Timelines (New
York, N.Y.)
E806.D83　　　　　1989　　　　　973.917—dc20　　　　　89-34401
　　　　　　　　　　　　　　　　　　　　　　　　　　　　　　　　　　　CIP
　　　　　　　　　　　　　　　　　　　　　　　　　　　　　　　　　　　AC

Photo credits
Cover: The Bettmann Archive: One of the many women who worked in American
　　factories during World War II
FPG International: 4, 9, 15, 16 (left), 20, 35
Wide World Photos: 7, 10, 11, 12, 16 (right), 17, 18, 21, 23, 24, 25, 27, 28, 29, 30, 31, 33, 36, 38,
　　39, 41, 43, 45
The Bettmann Archive: 14, 26, 46

Copyright © 1989 by Crestwood House, Macmillan Publishing Company

Macmillan Publishing Company
866 Third Avenue
New York, NY 10022
Collier Macmillan Canada, Inc.

CRESTWOOD HOUSE

Produced by Carnival Enterprises

Printed in the United States of America

First Edition

10　9　8　7　6　5　4　3　2　1

CONTENTS

INTRODUCTION

The 1940s started with economic depression and a war raging in Europe. Americans were jumping, jiving, and jitterbugging. But the dark days of World War II came to the states in 1941 when Japanese bombs destroyed Pearl Harbor, Hawaii. Men, and some women, went off to war. Women who stayed home took over men's jobs. Government agencies fixed wages and rents and were on the lookout for spies. Meat, coffee, butter, and shoes were scarce, but jobs were not. Along with war came prosperity for Americans. We still hear names of forties movie stars: Humphrey Bogart and Lauren Bacall, Frank Sinatra, Bette Davis, Spencer Tracy and Katharine Hepburn, James Stewart, Judy Garland, Marlene Dietrich, and others. Franklin Delano Roosevelt, a beloved president, did not live to see the end of the war. Spirits revived when it was over. Soldiers came home, and families gathered in living rooms where TV promised to be a new favorite. The Soviet Union and the United States were the only world powers intact. The United Nations was formed in the hopes of lasting world peace. It was a decade when even comic book characters were busy keeping the world safe, fighting for "truth, justice, and the American way."

Adolf Hitler, the führer of Germany and leader of the Nazi party, led the world into a second major war.

1940

A NICKEL A TUNE

Five cents was all you needed to have hit tunes at your fingertips. In the 1940s the nickel jukebox appeared in taverns, tea rooms, and variety stores. They were also put in gas stations, restaurants, and barbershops. Sixteen records cost 50 cents. But that's not all you could select from a jukebox. Three minutes of silence were available for a nickel, too!

TUNE IN TO SUPERMAN

The Man of Steel had already been fighting crime for two years in Action Comics. In 1940, he became the star of his own radio program. It was in the radio program—not in the comic book—that Kryptonite came into the story. Superman could fly faster than a speeding bullet. He could leap tall buildings in a single bound. The only thing Superman didn't have was a human weakness. The radio show gave it to him: Superman was in trouble if he got near Kryptonite. A rock from the planet he was born on, Kryptonite could rob Superman of his strength. After Kryptonite was introduced, Superman had some close calls. But he always managed to triumph.

"WHAT'S UP, DOC?"

Bugs Bunny made his first cartoon appearance in 1940. He has been in theaters ever since. Bugs munched his way through stolen carrots as he defied his enemy, Elmer Fudd. Since rabbits can't talk, Bugs's voice was borrowed from a man named Mel Blanc. It was Mel who said, "Well . . . ah . . . What's up, Doc?" Unfortunately, Mel Blanc was allergic to carrots. He tried making Bugs's munching noises with turnips, apples, and celery. But nothing sounded like the real thing. So Mel had to use real carrots. He munched then quickly spit them out.

Bugs Bunny began entertaining kids in 1940.

6

1940

NO WAY

Do you believe everything you read in encyclopedias? This story might make you think twice!

British novelist Alec Waugh had wanted to visit the West Indian island of Saba ever since he had read about it in the *Encyclopaedia Britannica*. The article had stirred his curiosity. It said that because there were no beaches in Saba, "the finest boatmakers in the Caribbean" had to lower their boats over the side of a cliff. Since Saba was difficult to get to, Waugh relied on the article for facts when he wrote a book about the West Indies. After the book was published, a reader told Waugh there was "no truth whatsoever" to what he wrote about Saba! The reader then told Waugh about a story in the November 1940 issue of *National Geographic*. The article, by Charles W. Herbert, claimed that Saba had no natural timber. It also said no boats were made there and that islanders could never have lifted massive logs up to the top of the cliff, built boats, and then lowered the boats down to the water. The cliff was 1,500 feet high.

Waugh didn't believe it until he checked it out for himself. He visited Saba and talked to some of its oldest residents. None of them could remember a time when boats were lowered over the cliff by ropes. In a later book, Alec Waugh wrote: "I am convinced that Mr. Herbert was right and that the encyclopedia was wrong."

FIRSTS IN FORTY

Nickel jukeboxes are a thing of the past. But we're still enjoying other new things from 1940. Morton Salt is one. It was also the year that gave us the first synthetic rubber tire as well as synthetic tooth fillings. Shoppers at Tiffany's enjoyed the first fully air-conditioned store. And travelers relaxed in more comfort on the first commercial flights with pressurized cabins.

CARTOONS AND CAMOUFLAGE

The jeep could climb hills, ford streams, and cut through the deep and sticky mud of war zones. Soldiers soon relied upon this powerful, open-topped, four-seat vehicle that could go anywhere. The jeep made its debut on November 11, 1940. Its name, some say, comes from the sound of the first letters of "general purpose." Others say soldiers named the rugged little machine after a popular cartoon character. Eugene the Jeep had appeared in the Popeye cartoon strip as a tough little dog who survived many trials and troubles. Soldiers admired his toughness. They also liked the fact that Eugene could become invisible—a highly prized state to be in when dodging the bullets of war.

This jeep is being taken on a test run on an army base in Georgia. Soldiers were impressed by the jeep's ability to go almost anywhere and to lay smoke screens that could hide troops.

1941

PLUNGED INTO WAR

Japanese bombers shattered the Sunday morning peace and quiet of Pearl Harbor, Hawaii, on December 7, 1941. The attack wiped out half of the United States Pacific Fleet. More than 3,700 Americans died. The attack meant the end of peace for the next 1,364 days. The United States had been forced to enter the war.

Many Americans remember where they were when the bombs fell. It was a shocking moment and impossible to forget. The news flashed across the country's airwaves. And in Pearl Harbor, the scene was one of fire, destruction, and death. Doctors appealed for blood to help the wounded. Within an hour,

The destroyer U.S.S. Shaw *exploding at Pearl Harbor after being hit by Japanese bombers*

Many U.S. Air Force planes and buildings were destroyed in the attack at Pearl Harbor as well.

500 volunteers were at the door of the Honolulu blood bank. The hospital ran out of containers. Doctors and nurses used sterilized Coke bottles to collect blood donations.

World War II changed life for almost everyone. New factories were built. Synthetic rubber and plastics were developed. More than 27 million people moved during the war. Farm workers left farms for business and factory jobs in the North or in newly booming southern cities. Industries and people spread west-ward to the Pacific coast. They started a population trend that still continues. Thousands of men were drafted into the armed forces. Women joined up, too. Sweethearts quickly married before husbands left for the war. Three million children were born each year in the baby boom of 1942 and 1943. Service wives set up housekeeping in new parts of the country to be near their husbands. When the men went to war, the women took jobs. They made bullets and riveted planes, tanks, and ships. People talked about "juvenile delinquency" more often as younger and younger children roamed the streets while their mothers worked.

With so many workers, war production zoomed to new heights. People made more money than ever before. They spent more, too, in nightclubs and restaurants. They bought luxuries like fur coats and jewelry. Movie stars such as Bing Crosby, Frank Sinatra, Dorothy Lamour, and Jane Wyman lent glamour to war-bond rallies. They drew crowds and urged the people to buy war bonds to help finance the war.

Men and women prepare a dive bomber for its paint job.

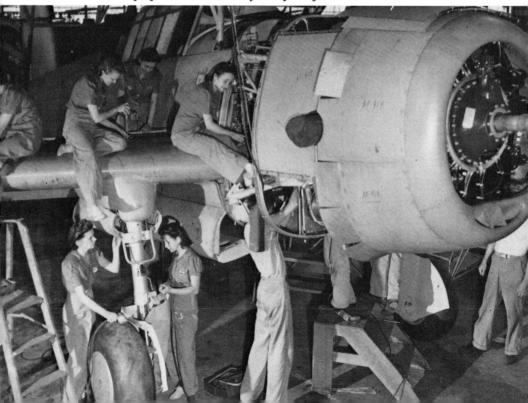

THE BEAT GOES ON

War time or not, music and movies were part of the scene. "Chattanooga Choo-Choo" was the song on everyone's lips in 1941. Some top movies were Orson Welles's *Citizen Kane*, Alfred Hitchcock's *Suspicion, The Big Store* with the Marx Brothers, and *Two-Faced Woman* with Greta Garbo.

SLIMY SLIM

What would you call a serpent that was 50 feet long with a head like a snub-nosed crocodile? Thomas L. Rogers of Boise, Idaho, called it Slimy Slim. He wasn't the only one in Boise who claimed to see the creature. Several other people reported seeing it as well. They all agreed on the description. It's strange, but Slimy Slim hasn't been seen, dead or alive, since 1941.

A SUPERHERO BECOMES A SUPERSTAR

In 1941, Superman came out of the comics pages and the radio airwaves and onto the movie screen. The first Superman movie was an animated cartoon. The same year, 200,000 children joined the Superman of America fan club. One dime bought a membership certificate, a Superman button, and a secret Superman code. The first of the superheroes would be around for many more years!

JOE DIMAGGIO HAS A BAD DAY

The New York Yankees' outfielder Joe DiMaggio was on his famous batting streak. He had had good hits in 56 straight games. But on May 30, Joe messed up. In a doubleheader against the Boston Red Sox, Joe misplayed a ground ball. Then he dropped a fly ball. While trying to throw runners out at the plate, he heaved the ball all the way into the grandstand . . . twice! It was one of the worst streaks of fielding foul-ups in baseball.

HE'S A GOOD GIRL!

He barked too much. He disturbed the neighbors. How could such a bad-mannered dog earn millions of dollars for movies and TV?

The dog's owner brought the difficult collie, named Pal, to dog training school. He hoped the dog could be broken of the bad barking habit. Finally, Pal's owner gave up, and the trainer, Rudd Weatherwax, became Pal's new owner. He trained the dog well.

In 1942, he got a chance to show how well.

That summer, a movie called *Lassie Come Home* was being filmed. But when the star started shedding, she didn't look good enough for the part. Along came Rudd Weatherwax with his

A collie named Pal rose to fame playing Lassie in a movie that costarred Roddy McDowell.

Japanese Americans were forced to live in internment camps during World War II.

sleek male collie, Pal. The rest is show biz history. Even though the role calls for a girl, Pal got the part.

Pal became Lassie, the dog who could do anything. In his movies, he rescued people from burning houses, evil villains, and terrible floods. Pal's children, grandchildren, and even great, great, great grandchildren have all played Lassie!

SAD BUT TRUE

Americans reacted to Hitler's conquest of Europe with fear that sometimes neared panic. After the Japanese bombing of Pearl Harbor, Americans were more afraid. They turned on Japanese Americans with anger and violence. Many Japanese Americans lived on the west coast, particularly in California. In February, the president let the army control civilian affairs in those states. Shortly after, thousands of Japanese-American men, women, and children were rounded up. They were herded into camps surrounded by barbed wire and guards.

1942

IT'S A KEEPER!

What's the best-selling record of all time? The 1942 recording of "White Christmas" sung by Bing Crosby. Crosby's version has sold more than 25 million copies. Almost everyone has heard it. But not everyone knows the country's most popular song spent three years in a trunk.

When Irving Berlin wrote "White Christmas" in 1939, he didn't think much of it. Luckily, he tossed it into a trunk instead of a trash can. He forgot about it until he needed it for a Bing Crosby-Fred Astaire movie called *Holiday Inn*. At first Crosby didn't want to sing the song. He felt the song missed the true meaning of Christmas. But he finally agreed to take 18 minutes to make the recording. It soon became an all-time hit. Over the years, "White Christmas" has appeared in 550 versions, selling six million copies of sheet music and 136,260,000 records—in the United States and Canada alone.

FLASHY THREADS

If you had been a young man in 1942, you might have worn a zoot suit. It was the male fashion rage of the early war years in the United States. The legs of the pants bagged below the knees.

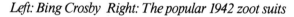

Left: Bing Crosby Right: The popular 1942 zoot suits

The cuffs were pulled tightly around the ankles. To look really fashionable, a man added a chain and a wide-brimmed hat or a long jacket and fancy suspenders. Some people thought the outfits were bizarre. They said wearing a zoot suit was more like a stunt than a fashion statement. There were even riots against the zoot suit in New York and California!

YO! JOE!

G. I. Joe first appeared in a comic strip in *Yank* magazine on June 17, 1942. America had just entered World War II. G. I. Joe was a "real American hero." He was dressed in camouflage fatigues and fighting gear. He gave people hope in an uneasy time.

BAMBI

Bambi arrived at movie theaters in 1942. The movie had only about 900 words but had taken five years to produce. Walt Disney wanted to get every detail right. Live animals were brought into the studio so artists could study their movements. The artists could then make better drawings and make the animations look more realistic. A crew was sent to Maine to study the animals' natural habitat. They also worked hard on the scenes with songs. In the "Little April Shower" scene, for instance, the audience sees close-ups of raindrops falling and splattering. Woodwinds provide the sound effects. Those things took time to create and produce. But the results were worth it. *Bambi* gave us a gentle story about the cycle of life in the forest. And it gave us characters that captured our hearts. Thumper the Rabbit, Flower the Skunk, and, of course, Bambi will be around for years.

Bambi and his friends Thumper and Flower

1943

SHORT SUPPLIES

How would you like it if the government said you could only have three pairs of shoes a year? That's what happened during World War II. Shoe rationing began early in 1943. The supply of leather had run low. Canned goods were the next items to be rationed, joining shoes, coffee, and sugar. Things that were needed for war supplies or materials were rationed or handed out in limited quantity. Shoes, coffee, and sugar could still be purchased, but only with stamps from special ration books. When people paid for things with stamps rather than money, the government could control supplies of scarce items. Folks at home had to get along with less during the war, but they knew it was for a good cause.

Food is rationed out to a crowd, many of whom had been waiting overnight.

BOFF! THWAPP! ZOWEE!

The Masked Manhunter and the Boy Wonder, Robin, joined the newspapers in a comic strip in 1943.

The superpowerful and supersmart Batman lived in his lab, the Batcave. He drove his Batmobile, owned a Batplane, and lassoed criminals with a Batarang. Robin had a motorcycle. He also had crimefighting tools in his belt. His famous words were, "If this doesn't work, they'll be having shredded crimebuster for breakfast!"

Batman is still fighting criminals today. So we can still hear the bat-noises of the old-time comic book hero: EEE-YOW! BOFF! THWAPP! ZOWIE! SWOOSH! KLONK! SPLATT! AARGH!

TEEN TALK

What did teenagers do in 1943? One idea they came up with was the slumber party. Kids liked to "mess around" the soda shop on Saturday night, listening to the jukebox. They "smooched" in jalopies. They lived it up at pep rallies, beach parties, and roller rinks. Girls wore their boyfriends' jackets. They knitted argyle socks and met their dates at hamburger joints.

WHAT'S THE COST?

In 1943, a talking doll cost $5.95. If starting an aquarium was your dream, you'd spend 49 cents for a two-gallon fish tank and five cents for each guppy and snail. Angelfish and tetras went for twelve cents each. Postcards were a penny, and airmail postage cost eight cents.

Many jobs were filled by women when the majority of men went to fight in World War II.

THAT'S TEAMWORK!

By 1943, half of the workers on assembly lines were women. Men and women stood side by side. They worked so well together that they could build an entire cargo ship in 17 days. At one point, America had built such an enormous storehouse of arms that the government said "Enough!" Some factories were ordered to cut back production for a while. All Americans felt they were a part of the war effort. They worked hard and were proud to help.

Volunteers formed Civil Defense Corps. Air spotters watched the skies for enemy planes. Air raid wardens enforced blackouts.

Americans grew their own food in "victory gardens." In 1943 alone, these "Sunday farmers" produced one-third of all fresh vegetables consumed in the United States.

Americans went on wartime scavenger hunts to find materials needed for war items. Women turned in their silk and nylon stockings to make powder bags for naval guns. Children saved their empty toothpaste tubes for scrap-metal drives. This "junk" was made into weapons. An old radiator yielded enough steel for 17 rifles. One lawn mower was turned into six 3-inch shells. One old rubber tire became twelve gas masks. Even bacon grease was taken back to the butcher. It was used in making explosives. By 1945, this salvage was supplying the steel and tin needed to win the war.

1943

Many Americans planted victory gardens to help the war effort. The profits from this garden went to an organization that helped American officers.

COMIC HEROES HELP THE WAR

The American funny papers went to the war with American soldiers. Daddy Warbucks from the *Little Orphan Annie* comic strip served as a general. His adopted orphan, Annie, reminded her young readers to collect scrap metal. Joe Palooka was a nice-guy character created by Ham Fisher. When Joe joined the army in his comic strip, the number of Americans who enlisted zoomed. President Franklin D. Roosevelt personally thanked Mr. Fisher for Joe's military service. Superman, however, stayed home from war. Believe it or not, the Man of Steel was ruled 4-F, or not acceptable for military duty. Why? He flunked his army physical because his X-ray vision betrayed him. Without realizing it, Superman looked right through the eye chart and the wall. He read the letters on another chart in the next room! Rejected, he spent the war promoting the Red Cross and selling war bonds.

TAKE YOUR TIME

Do you like ketchup on your burger and fries? Heinz was thinking about your ketchup tastes long before squeeze bottles and take-out windows. In 1944, a 14-ounce bottle was introduced. It is identical to the one we use today! Actually, over the last 100 years, the basic design of the ketchup bottle has changed only a little. When Heinz ketchup was first introduced, it was thin and runny. The ketchup came in an octagonal bottle with a narrow neck to "slow the flow."

THE PENINSULA PYTHON

Clarence Mitchell of Peninsula, Ohio, was the first to see it. He was in his cornfield down by the swamp on June 8, 1944. An 18-foot python crawled silently along the ground where Clarence was hoeing. A few days later a woman gathering eggs from

Joe Palooka (left) knocked out many opponents in his comic strip before enlisting in the army in 1944.

her henhouse spotted the python. It was climbing over a wire fence. A big bulge in its middle was a clue that one of her chickens had been its lunch. Townspeople guessed the snake came from a carnival truck that had crashed two years earlier. A lot of picnics were called off as dozens of other people saw the 250-pound snake. It became known as the Peninsula Python. Cold weather that fall ended the sightings.

DISNEY WAR HEROES

During the war, Disney Studio spent 90 percent of its time and money on war-related projects. Mickey, Donald, and other characters were painted on jeeps, trucks, tanks, and aircraft. Walt Disney made training films for the army, navy, and other government agencies. *Food Will Win the War, Four Methods of Flush Riveting,* and *Stop That Tank* were some of the titles. They weren't big attractions like *Dumbo* or *Bambi,* but they carried important messages to those who viewed them.

On June 6, 1944, Allied Forces surprised the Germans with a landing at Normandy. The password for the mission was "Mickey Mouse."

The landing at Normandy from the soldiers' point of view

Although it came as a surprise, Walt Disney was also an important part of the secret D-Day invasion. The invasion involved soldiers, sailors, and airmen and thousands of tanks and guns. The plan went into action on June 6, 1944, D-Day. Under the command of General Dwight Eisenhower, Allied Forces landed at Normandy on the coast of France. Between dawn and dusk, about 176,000 men splashed ashore.

The invasion at Normandy was a turning point in World War II. It caught the Germans completely off guard. The following May, Germany surrendered, ending the war in Europe.

Walt Disney himself was in New York during the invasion. But government officials called him to tell him the Allied forces were invading at Normandy. They also let him know that the password for the invasion was "Mickey Mouse."

TEENAGE MOVIE STAR

You didn't have to love horses to love Elizabeth Taylor in *National Velvet*. The 1945 film was a big success. Taylor was only 13 years old when she made it. She's still a celebrity today.

A DIARY THAT BECAME FAMOUS

A young German-Jewish girl named Anne Frank and her family lived secretly in a small, dark attic for two years. Their hideout was located over an office building in Amsterdam, Holland. Anne's family and other Jews had been forced into hiding. It was the only chance they had of escaping persecution by Hitler's Nazis during World War II. Thousands of Jews had already been killed by the Nazis.

The hidden family had to be quiet during the daytime. That's when the chances of discovery were greatest. To help pass time,

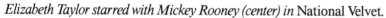

Elizabeth Taylor starred with Mickey Rooney (center) in National Velvet.

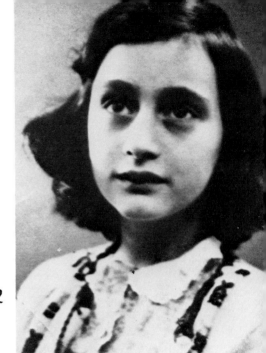

Dit is een foto, zoals
ik me zou wensen,
altijd zo te zijn.
Dan had ik nog wel
een kans om naar
Holywood te komen.
Anne Frank.
10 Oct. 1942

A photo of Anne Frank and a section taken from her diary. The section reads: "This is a photo as I would wish myself to look all the time. Then I would maybe have a chance to come to Hollywood."

Anne spent many hours writing a diary. She wrote about herself, her family, and her feelings. Sadly, Anne and her family were betrayed and discovered. They were sent to a concentration camp. In March 1945, starved and feverish, Anne rolled off her bunk and fell lifeless to the floor. She was 16 years old. Only Anne's father survived. Just weeks later, the war ended. The gates of the Nazi death camps were opened by Allied soldiers. The surviving Jews were freed.

The woman who had hidden the Franks found the scraps of paper and books on which Anne wrote her diary. She gave it to Anne's father after he was released. It was published in 1947. One of the last things Anne wrote was her belief that all people are good. Anne's diary has served as an example of human courage. It is a reminder of the horrors of the Holocaust.

TOP ROCKET SPECIALIST SURRENDERS

Germany had produced many excellent scientists during the war. One of them, Wernher von Braun, had started to work on a rocket that would send people to the moon. In 1945, von Braun surrendered to the Allied troops in Austria. Von Braun was taken to the United States where he continued his research. Twenty-four years later, his research gave us the giant rocket that landed American astronauts on the moon.

ROOSEVELT'S DEATH STUNS THE WORLD

On April 12, 1945, one of the most remarkable presidents in history died suddenly. Franklin Delano Roosevelt served as president for more than 12 years. He led the United States through its worst depression and through its worst war. Unfortunately, he did not live to see the end of the war. Germany did not surrender until May, 1945. Japan's surrender did not come until August.

Senator Robert Taft had often been FDR's political foe. But he was one of many who called Roosevelt the greatest figure of our time. He said the president died a hero of the war. He had worked himself to death in the service of the American people.

Winston Churchill, the British prime minister, and Mrs. Eleanor Roosevelt stand quietly by the grave of Franklin Roosevelt.

Left: The ruins of Hiroshima, Japan
Right: Smoke column from the atomic bomb dropped on Nagasaki, Japan

THE TOUGHEST DECISION

When President Roosevelt died, Vice President Harry Truman became president. The first major decision President Truman had to make was one of the most important in modern history. Truman had to decide if the atomic bomb should be dropped on Japan. He believed the powerful bomb could save lives by making Japan surrender and end the war. But no one was sure what the long-term effects of an atomic bomb would be. After great worry, Truman made the hard decision. On August 6, an atomic bomb was dropped on the city of Hiroshima, Japan. Three days later another was dropped on Nagasaki.

Between 80,000 and 100,000 in Hiroshima and 40,000 in Nagasaki were killed immediately. Thousands more were wounded and died later from burns. Japan surrendered. World War II, which had lasted almost six years, was over. The Nuclear Age had begun.

THE SECRET IS OUT

Three "hidden cities" with a total population of 100,000 were built to produce the atomic bomb. Secrecy was so great that workers were never even told what they were making. The vast factories covered many square miles in New Mexico.

29

THE COMPUTER AGE ARRIVES

Some scientists may have imagined using computers, but nobody had one. That is, not until 1946. The world's first electronic computer was named ENIAC. It worked by the flow of electrons in 18,000 vacuum tubes. It had 70,000 transistors and 6,000 switches. ENIAC weighed 30 tons and was about the size of a gymnasium. The United States Army used ENIAC to determine the path of bullets and bombs.

No one in 1946 could have predicted what the age of computers would bring. Today we have computers in businesses, homes, and schools. They fit onto desks, laps, and even into pockets! What next? That's probably what people said in 1946!

A whole room was needed to store all the parts of the ENIAC computer.

Ethel Merman as Annie Oakley

A SURE SHOT

Annie Oakley could shoot a hole in a playing card in midair while standing 90 feet away. That was part of her act in Buffalo Bill's Wild West Show in the 1880s and 1890s. She also inspired Irving Berlin to write a musical about her. Berlin's musical *Annie Get Your Gun* opened in New York on May 16 with Ethel Merman as Annie. One of the more popular songs was "There's No Business Like Show Business." The booming voice and personality of Ethel Merman made the play a hit. One reviewer wrote, "If Ethel Merman were a rifle and a song were a bullet, she could make bull's-eyes on a target clear across the Atlantic."

WHERE THERE'S SMOKE . . .

Scientists first discussed the possibility that cigarette smoking could harm a person's health at a meeting in October 1946. In fact, they said smoking might cause cancer. This news created quite a stir, and we haven't heard the last of it yet!

SOMETHING FOR COPY CATS

Chester F. Carlson knew he had a good idea. Others weren't so sure, however. First, Kodak turned it down. Then, the IBM Corporation rejected it twice. Finally, in 1946, the nearly bankrupt Haloid Corporation took a chance and invested in it. The company believed Chester Carlson's invention would be a money-maker. It was. Carlson was the inventor of xerography. Today, the Haloid Corporation is the Xerox Corporation. The story proves a good invention is worth pursuing. Chester Carlson did. Now millions of people can instantly make copies of any documents they need.

"ZIP-A-DEE-DOO-DAH"

You can probably hum a few bars of this tune. Maybe you can sing the whole song. The Oscar-winning song was from the biggest movie of this era, Walt Disney's *Song of the South*. Most of us have been charmed by the wily Brer Rabbit, the cunning Brer Fox, and the slow-witted Brer Bear. They were characters created by a storyteller named Uncle Remus. Thanks to new techniques Disney Studios had been working on for years, they became movie stars as well. For one of the first times, Disney paired live action with animation. That's why Uncle Remus can venture into Brer Rabbit's animated world singing "Zip-a-Dee-Doo-Dah."

MEAT CRISIS

This wasn't the year to be hungry for pot roast. Faced with a meat shortage, many Americans started eating horse meat. Beef, pork, and chicken were in short supply. The government had fixed monthly production quotas for slaughterhouses. But President Truman ordered the rules changed on October 15. Before long, farmers increased shipments of livestock. Fresh meat was back in the stores.

Longer skirts came back into style after World War II.

SKIRTS SWING AGAIN

Now that the war was over, longer skirts were legal again. Does that sound strange to you? During wartime, fabric was needed for parachutes, uniforms, and other war items. Short skirts used less fabric, so hems went up. On October 19, order L85 was repealed. That meant more fabric was available. Once again, women began wearing long, full skirts that swirled around their knees!

1947

A HOT-SELLING NEW TOY

In 1943, Richard James invented a small coiled wire toy that slunk around by the force of gravity. It even went down stairs by itself, end over end. His wife, Betty, thought it would make a good toy. She tried to interest people in it but had no luck. The war was still on, and wire was too precious to be used for toys. After World War II ended, Betty talked Gimbel's department store into displaying "Slinky" while she tried to sell it. Within 90 minutes, all 400 Slinkies she had were gone! On March 4, 1947, Mr. and Mrs. James obtained a patent, which gave them the sole right to make Slinkies. The next year, Slinkies were so popular that a floor at Macy's department store was jammed with people who had to have the new toy.

WAS HE HORSING AROUND?

In 1947, a famous horse race announcer named Clem McCarthy made a famous blooper. McCarthy was broadcasting to radio listeners all over the United States when he announced that a horse called Faultless had won the Preakness Stakes. It was the wrong horse! Jet Pilot was the real winner. Oops!

START FOR A STAR

He was the grandson of a slave. He was pigeon-toed and had ankle problems. But Jackie Robinson turned out to be one of the best athletes in America. He was also the first black baseball player in the major leagues. He joined the Brooklyn Dodgers in 1947.

When he began playing, Robinson had to put up with jeers and humiliating racism. Once, the Ku Klux Klan threatened to shoot Jackie before an Atlanta ballgame. But he didn't let that stop him. Robinson showed courage on and off the playing field.

Jackie Robinson

His acceptance opened the way for other black players. Many of them became baseball's greatest stars. In 1962, Jackie became the first black to be elected to the Baseball Hall of Fame. By the end of his playing career, Jackie Robinson had stolen twice as many bases as anyone else in the National League.

1947

1947

MYSTERIES IN THE SKY

Flying saucers were first reported flying over Mount Rainier, Washington, on June 24, 1947. "It must be your imagination," said many people. Others, including pilots, police officers, and church leaders, were convinced they saw unidentified flying objects—UFOs. That first sighting was the start of something big. During the 1950s, people reported an average of 600 UFO sightings a year. The United States Air Force spent $60,000 a year investigating them. But they still cannot say what in the world—or out of this world—they are.

SONIC BOOM!

Captain Charles ("Chuck") Yeager was definitely in a hurry. He wanted to be the first person to break the sound barrier. On October 14, 1947, he reached his goal. He was strapped into the bullet-shaped XS-1 research rocket plane and dropped from the belly of the B-29 mothership. Down . . . down . . . down Chuck fell. Then, whoosh! The rocket switch ignited. The plane accelerated. Yeager was flying at 670 miles per hour. Supersonic! He was going faster than the speed of sound.

MAKE IT RAIN!

December is warm and dry in parts of Nevada. In December 1947, the Rocking F Ranch laid claim to the water in all clouds passing over it. How did they plan to get the water? Seeding clouds was the answer. Also called rainmaking, cloud seeding is a process that makes rain fall from clouds. It was developed by several United States scientists in the 1940s. Cloud seeding not only made rain fall, but also stirred up opinions about the fairness of rainmaking. Not everyone could afford to "buy" rain. By the mid-1970s, laws had to be written to control rainmaking. In some states, it was outlawed.

THE DOODYVILLE GANG

Howdy Doody was the first great puppet of the television age. Starting in 1947, Howdy Doody time (5:30 P.M.) brought peace and quiet to households all over the United States. Children loved the friendly looking cowpoke puppet. They laughed with his pals—Dilly Dally, Flub-a-Dub, and Phineas T. Bluster. There were lovable humans on the show, too—Buffalo Bob, Clarabell the Clown, and Princess Summerfallwinterspring. But trouble was brewing for Doodyville. NBC faced a lawsuit and loss of the rights to Howdy Doody. A facelift would solve the problem. In 1948, Howdy got a new freckled face with blinking eyes and a snub nose. He also got red hair.

The audience was told Howdy was getting a new look so he could defeat Mr. X, the handsomest man in the world. Mr. X and Howdy were campaigning to become "President of All the Boys." It was the same year President Harry Truman was running for re-election. Howdy Doody won his campaign, too. As for NBC, it never feared losing Howdy again. He was popular with children until the mid-1950s.

Chuck Yeager

1948

GREAT TEACHER KILLED

Mahatma means great teacher. On January 30, 1948, Mohandas K. Gandhi was killed by an assassin's bullet in New Delhi, India. Mahatma Gandhi was a humble and gentle Hindu. He led a nonviolent "war" against the British in order to regain independence for India. His death was mourned around the world. But his teaching lived on.

MOTHER TERESA BEGINS HER WORK

In August 1948, Mother Teresa put on a white and blue sari and stepped across the threshold of a Catholic convent. She had chosen to leave her clean, peaceful home for the dirty, noisy streets of Calcutta, India. In Calcutta, many families lived and died on the streets. Their homes, made of mud or gasoline cans covered in burlap, gave little protection from heavy rains. For more than 40 years, Mother Teresa worked tirelessly for the poor. She set up hospitals and shelters. She set up a village for lepers.

Mother Teresa

In 1979, Mother Teresa was awarded the Nobel Peace Prize for the work she began in 1948. She will always be a powerful example of what one person can do to help others.

STICK TO IT!

Have you ever walked out of the woods on a fall day and found prickly burrs stuck to your socks? You're not the only one! In 1948, George de Mestral, a Swiss mountaineer, returned from a hunting trip and found his clothes covered with cockleburs. Examining the burrs under a microscope, he marveled at their design. The burrs were designed to stick to things that would carry them off and spread their seeds. Although burrs can be a nuisance to walkers, pets, and hunters, they gave George de Mestral an idea.

Perhaps people could make a fabric that would stick to another material the ways burrs do. Imagine—no zippers, buttons,

Mohandas Gandhi (right) and Jawaharlal Nehru attend the 1946 session of the All-India Congress committee meeting.

1948

hooks, or snaps! For ten years the Swiss mountaineer worked on the idea. He named his product Velcro. Today we use Velcro in clothing, sports, and even in the space program. Velcro is also popular as a shoe fastener. Many young children don't have to learn to tie shoelaces! De Mestral showed us we can look to nature for answers. The cocklebur created a $100 million industry.

A SNAPPY TALE

Farmer Gale Harris liked the large lake on his land in Churubusco, Indiana. The lake was great for his thirsty cows. It attracted flocks of feeding ducks. That's the way things went before 1948. Nice and peaceful. But then some strange things started happening. A cow went to the lake to drink and simply disappeared. Hoofprints led up to the edge of the water, but no hoofprints led away. Fish and ducks disappeared also. Something had killed them. Something with a big appetite.

The something was discovered to be a giant-sized snapping turtle. Those who saw the turtle said he was as big as a table. The turtle was named Oscar and people came from all over to try to catch him. They went after Oscar with nets, traps, hooks, and even guns, but Oscar eluded them all. Finally one day Harris found Oscar asleep in the sun. After slipping a chain around the turtle's middle, he attached the other end of the chain to four strong horses. But while the horses pulled with all their might, Oscar used his giant claws to dig into the ground. The tug-of-war ended when the chain broke and Oscar slid back into his watery hiding place.

The small town of Churubusco remembers Oscar every year with a special Turtle Days Festival. They make T-shirts with turtle logos, turtle-shaped candy, and toy turtles. Even though Oscar hasn't been seen for a while, no one celebrates with a swim in Harris Lake.

President Truman triumphantly holds up the Chicago Daily Tribune *that said he had lost the election.*

DON'T BELIEVE EVERYTHING YOU READ

One of the most embarrassing mistakes in newspaper history happened the morning after the 1948 presidential election. The *Chicago Daily Tribune* hit the newsstands with the headline DEWEY DEFEATS TRUMAN. Many opinion polls predicted that New York Governor Thomas E. Dewey would defeat Truman. But Truman and the voters surprised them all. The headline was printed before all the votes were in. One famous picture shows a victorious Harry Truman holding up the incorrect newspaper. He had the last laugh.

CHRISTMAS PRESENTS FROM THE SKY

A real Santa came to the German city of Berlin in December 1948. For months, all the roads and rail lines to Berlin had been blocked by the Soviet leader, Stalin. American and British pilots had been flying in food and coal for the German people. In the United States Air Force, First Lieutenant Carol F. Halvorson parachuted bags of candy and toys to the Berlin children who gathered each day to watch the planes roar in. The idea caught on. That Christmas pilots dropped thousands of parachutes with gifts. They bought the gifts with their own money. Thanks to American and British pilots, Stalin's blockade of Berlin failed. It was ended before the next Christmas came.

1948

POSSIBLE SNOW FLURRIES

Nobody, not even the Weather Bureau, knew it was coming. They reported "possible snow flurries." Whistling down from Alaska on January 2 came "snow flurries" that lasted seven straight weeks. It turned out to be the worst storm in history.

Wyoming and Colorado were hit first. The blizzard spread like a cold white blanket over North Dakota, South Dakota, and Montana. It crossed the Rockies and struck Utah, Idaho, and Nevada. It sent icy fingers down to sunny Arizona and New Mexico. It spread eastward into Kansas and Oklahoma. Houses were buried to the roof as the storm raged on. Blinded by snow, cattle crowded together and died.

By the middle of January, thousands of people were nearly without food. The strong winds blew powdery snow into cars and barns. Some livestock smothered in barns, buried under snow. Sheets of ice like iron covered feed supplies. Deer and elk, looking for food, flocked along the roads where snowplows had opened paths.

The blizzard blasted from January 2 to February 19. On 25 of the 48 days there were big storms. The temperature dropped to 50 degrees below zero.

Many tales of courage were told about rescue work. A bus driver named W. L. Owens saved many motorists. He found people asleep in cars and woke them up by slapping and rubbing them. On one of his rescue trips he had 96 people in a bus built for 40.

Air Force planes dropped food, blankets, and medical supplies to people, and feed for animals. Radio stations told people to signal for the airplanes with lines in the snow. A single line in the snow meant a doctor was needed. Two lines called for medicines. An "F" called for food. "L" stood for fuel. And "LL" meant "we're okay."

Luckily, the right kind of weather followed the blizzard. There were no floods, and the melting snow brought plenty of water for irrigation in the summer. In the Great Blizzard of '49, acts of human courage matched the power of nature.

PRESTO!

The Polaroid Land camera went on the market for $89.75. This new invention produced a picture in just 60 seconds.

TELEVISION RATES BIG

When the 40s began, television was new. World War II nearly stopped the growth of American TV. Electronics factories were needed for war arms and equipment. But when the war was over, TV production took off. In 1946, the United States government lifted its wartime ban on the manufacture of new sets. Between 1949 and 1951, the number of TV sets in America jumped from one million to more than ten million!

The army and the U.S. Indian Service join together to get medical aid to snowbound citizens during the Great Blizzard of '49.

1949

HOPALONG CASSIDY CASHES IN

Hopalong Cassidy bicycles with built-in holsters. Skates with spurs. Toy guns. Snowsuits and cowboy outfits. Rugs and bedspreads. Shirts, soaps, snacks, watches, and wallpaper. These items earned actor William Boyd more money than the royalties he received for playing the part of Hopalong Cassidy on television. A year earlier, in 1948, Boyd had bought the rights from Hopalong's creator. In 1949 and the early 1950s, he cashed in beyond his wildest dreams. What had William Boyd paid author Clarence Mulford? A mere $90.

CLOWNS COME TO THE COURT

They stood on each other's shoulders to make baskets. They hid basketballs under their shirts and pulled them out in time to swish through the rim. The tallest players held balls aloft on their fingertips, frustrating the defense into fouls. They stopped the play midquarter to tell the spectators a new joke. These were the antics of the Harlem Globetrotters. They entertained fans from all over the world with their mischief and skillful pranks. They were clowns. The Globetrotters were known for their comedy on the court, not for their serious ball playing.

Serious basketball in 1948 meant the Minneapolis Lakers, the champions of the National Basketball Association. Their success and skills had been unchallenged by any other team. But then someone proposed "the Pro Basketball Game of the Year." The Harlem Globetrotters would play the reigning champions, the Lakers. It was a close contest. But the Globetrotters scored the winning basket one second before the final buzzer. The two teams fought it out again in 1949. This time, the Globetrotters couldn't resist their usual clowning around. They won by only one point. Victory was sweet, but the Globetrotters probably could have turned a loss into a few smiles, too.

44

NOT SO SILLY

That bouncy toy, Silly Putty, was discovered by mistake. During World War II, some scientists were trying to create a synthetic rubber. When they accidentally dropped some boric acid into silicone oil, they suddenly had a strange new substance. It wasn't the substitute for rubber they were looking for. Still, they didn't throw it away. In 1949, American Paul Hodgson bought $147 worth of the soft, stretchy stuff from the scientists. He called it "Silly Putty" and sold it as a toy.

The Harlem Globetrotters and the Minneapolis Lakers play a close game of basketball.

After the war, many women continued to work in factories and offices throughout the United States.

INDEX